JUV 6910 KAL

Water

HEALTHY ME

Published by Smart Apple Media
1980 Lookout Drive, North Mankato, Minnesota 56003

Copyright © 2004 Smart Apple Media. International copyrights reserved in all countries.
No part of this book may be reproduced in any form without written permission from the publisher.

PHOTOGRAPHS BY Richard Cummins, Heartland Images (Paul T. McMahon), Unicorn Stock Photos
(Eric R. Berndt, Willard Griffin, B. W. Hoffmann, Wayne Floyd, Tom McCarthy, Marcia Pennington,
Gary Randall, Jim Shippee), Tom Stack & Associates (Ann Duncan, Novastock, Milton Rand,
Eric Sanford, Mark Allen Stack)
DESIGN BY Evansday Design

First Edition

9 8 7 6 5 4 3 2 1

Water

A World of Water

The world will never run out of water. Water can freeze and change to ice. Or it can get hot and change to steam. But the **amount** of water the world has today is the same amount that it had millions of years ago.

The water you drink once fell from the sky as rain. When it rains, water runs into lakes and rivers. Rivers carry the water to the ocean.

5

Water that falls from the sky is called rain. ⌃

< Rivers carry rainwater to the ocean.

The sun warms the water in the ocean. When water gets hot, it turns into steam. The steam from the ocean floats into the air and makes clouds. Soon rain falls from the clouds. This is called the water cycle.

Some of the water you drink may have been drunk by dinosaurs millions of years ago.

All clouds are made of water.

7

Drinking Water

Everybody needs water. You can live without food for about a month. But you cannot live without water for more than a few days.

Most people drink water from a **faucet**. This water is called tap water. Tap water comes from rivers or lakes. It can also come from underground. But before it gets to your faucet, tap water goes to a **treatment plant**.

Treatment plants make water safe to drink.

9

< Water from a faucet is called tap water.

People in a treatment plant clean water. They take out dirt and bugs. They kill germs. Then they send the clean water through underground pipes to your faucet.

Oceans cover most of the world. But we cannot drink ocean water because it is too salty.

Some people dig deep holes in the ground to get water. These holes are called wells.

Water and Your Body

More than half of your body is made of water.

There is water in your skin, eyes, nose, and ears.

Blood is made of water. So is **saliva**.

Your body needs water to do everything. It needs water to move your blood. To keep your brain and heart healthy. To move **vitamins** to different parts of your body. To move bad things, such as germs, out of your body. Without water, you could not cry or swallow. You could not go to the bathroom.

Your body needs water to make tears. ⌃

13

< Water helps keep your body healthy.

Water also keeps your body cool. Sweat is made of water. When you are hot, sweat comes out of your skin and makes it wet. Wet skin cools faster than dry skin.

Most treatment plants add fluoride to tap water. Fluoride makes teeth hard and strong.

Sweat keeps you from getting too hot.

Eating Right

Your body is always losing water. You lose water when you breathe. You lose water when you sweat and when you go to the bathroom. So it is important to drink water every day.

You can get water from milk or juice. Soup is mostly water. So are fruits and vegetables. All foods have some water in them. Even toast and cereal! But drinking water is best.

17

Apples have a lot of water in them.

< Some drinking water comes in bottles.

Eating healthy foods is important. Drinking water is even more important. Water is your body's best friend!

The water that goes down your sink or tub drain is cleaned and used again.

Camels can drink a tubful of water, then go a week without another drink.

Glasses of Water

20

Drinking water comes from many different places. This makes each kind of water look and taste a little different.

WHAT YOU NEED

Tap water from your house
Tap water from a friend's house
Bottled mineral water
Bottled purified water (non-carbonated)
Four clear glasses
A friend

WHAT YOU DO

1. Have your friend close his or her eyes. Then pour each kind of water into a different glass.
2. Now have your friend look at, smell, and taste each glass. Does one glass of water look better? Does one smell or taste bad? Which is your friend's favorite?

amount everything added up; how much

faucet a pipe with a set of handles or knobs that turn water on or off

saliva the watery liquid in your mouth; it is also called spit

treatment plant a place where water is made safe to drink

vitamins things in food that keep your body healthy and growing

Read More

Kerley, Barbara. *A Cool Drink of Water*. New York: National Geographic Society, 2002.

Lombardo, Michelle. *The Organ Wise Guys: Learning to Be Smart from the Inside Out*. Duluth, Ga.: Wellness, Inc., 1996.

Relf, Patricia. *The Magic School Bus Wet All Over: A Book About the Water Cycle*. New York: Scholastic, 1996.

Explore the Web

EPA: DRINKING WATER FOR KIDS

http://www.epa.gov/safewater/kids

KIDSHEALTH

http://kidshealth.org/kid/stay_healthy/food/water

NWWA KID ZONE: THE WATER WIZARD

http://www.nwwater.com/kidszone

23

blood 12, 13

drinking water 16, 17, 18

oceans 5, 6, 11

rain 5, 6

saliva 12

sweat 14, 16

tap water 9, 15

treatment plants 9–10, 15

water cycle 5–6

wells 11